Sea Monsters
Myth and Truth

M. J. Cosson

Perfection Learning®

About the Author

M. J. Cosson loves animals of all shapes and sizes. She also likes to scuba dive and explore ocean life.

Cover Image: Northwind Archives

Image Credits: AP Photo Archive p. 7 (top); Corbis/Bettmann pp. 10, 37 (top), 49; North Wind Picture Archives pp. 5 (top), 14; Charles Otway p. 11 (top); Jeffrey L. Rotman/Corbis p. 36 (left)

Art Today (images copyright www.arttoday.com) pp. 3, 4, 5 (bottom), 6, 8 (bottom), 9, 12, 13, 16, 17 (bottom), 18, 20, 21, 24, 25, 27, 28–29, 35, 39, 50, 52, 55; Corbis p. 22 (top); Corel pp. 7 (bottom), 8 (top), 30 (top), 32 (top), 33 (middle), 38 (top), 41, 42, 44 (bottom), 45, 46 (bottom), 47; M. J. Cosson p. 36 (right); Digital Stock pp. 22 (bottom), 30 (middle), 32 (bottom), 37 (bottom), 44 (top); Jerome Hamlin p. 11 (bottom); IMSI pp. 43 (top), 46 (top); NOAA pp. 15, 17 (top), 23, 26, 30 (bottom), 31, 33 (top, bottom), 34, 38 (bottom), 43 (bottom), 51

Perfection Learning® Corporation,
1000 North Second Avenue,
P.O. Box 500, Logan, Iowa 51546-0500.
Phone: 1-800-831-4190 • Fax: 1-712-644-2392
Paperback ISBN 0-7891-5047-6
Cover Craft® ISBN 0-7807-9013-8
4 5 6 7 8 PP 09 08 07 06

Table of Contents

Prologue

Sea monsters! These two words could strike terror in the hearts of most levelheaded people. That's because in the olden days—before today's technology—people thought sea creatures were monsters. You'll have to admit, there are some weird-looking things living in the ocean.

In olden days, how did people learn about these strange creatures? Sometimes, a huge, partly decomposed body washed up on shore. Local people gathered around. A museum **curator** might have been interested in displaying the corpse. That is, if it didn't stink too badly. Newspapers ran stories. They would quote local scientists and feature drawings or cartoons of the monster.

Sometimes, a ship set out for sea. It would never return. If no other ships were close by, there was no way of knowing what had happened. Did the ship sink in a storm? Was it swallowed by a **kraken**? Perhaps a **polyp** got it.

Some seafarers did make it home. They told tall tales about the sea. The terrors that hid underwater were not for the faint of heart. Only the bravest, most foolhardy sailors or those **shanghaied** ventured out to sea.

Compare the dark mysteries of yesterday with what we know now. Today, we have technology to help us explore the oceans. It helps us see into the dark depths, breathe underwater, and withstand the water pressure. And so, we finally are learning about sea animals' behavior. Sea monsters are losing their creepy qualities.

Nowadays, where do you go for a good scare? You probably head for the movies. Or you read a scary book. It's fun to be scared, isn't it?

Old stories and myths introduce some of the monsters in this book. To read these parts of this book, you need to let go of what you know. You need to go back in time. Pretend there is no TV, computer, microwave—not even a telephone or lightbulb in your house. Sit by the fire or find a bright whale-oil lamp. Pull your quilt over your shoulders and get cozy.

Imagine you are at a seaside cottage. It's a cold, stormy night. The wind is howling outside. The shutters are flapping against the outside walls. You can hear the waves crashing on the shore. Think of how big and powerful the sea is. And think of the mysterious monsters that lie beneath it.

Now you're ready to read this book.

CHAPTER 1

Nessie, Plesiosaurs, and Ichthyosaurs

Have you heard of the Loch Ness monster? It's probably the most famous monster in the world. Many articles and books have been written about it.

Loch means lake in Scottish. So the Loch Ness monster isn't really a sea monster at all.

Loch Ness is part of the Great Glen. It is a deep fault that cuts all the way across Scotland. Possibly at one time, the sea did extend into the loch.

The loch is dark and murky. Nothing can be seen below the surface. But many people claim to have seen something in the water.

The first recorded sighting of the Loch Ness monster was in the sixth century. A Scottish holy man, St. Columba, saw the great monster attack another man in the water. St. Columba yelled at the monster and drove it away.

Since then, hundreds of people have seen the monster. In fact, they fondly call it "Nessie." In most photos and drawings, Nessie has a long neck, large body, and small head.

Today, most scholars believe that the Loch Ness monster isn't real. Still, it seems strange that so many people claim to have seen it.

Scholars have noted that the Loch Ness monster looks very much like plesiosaurs (PLEE see uh sorz) or ichthyosaurs (IK thee uh sorz). If not now, maybe hundreds of years ago, a survivor of the dinosaur age did live in Loch Ness.

As far as we know, plesiosaurs lived from 195 to 65 million years ago. They lived during the **Jurassic period**. But they were not related to dinosaurs. They were **marine reptiles**.

In Greek, *plesiosaur* means "near lizard." Some plesiosaurs swallowed small stones. They probably did this to help themselves dive deep in the water or to help grind their food.

Plesiosaurs grew to 40 feet long. They had broad bodies, medium tails, long, snaky necks, and small heads.

Plesiosaurs' large front and back flippers were strong. They moved quickly through water, much like marine turtles do.

Needlelike teeth tell us that these creatures were probably **predators**.

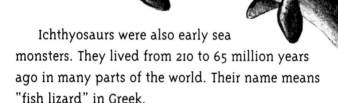

Ichthyosaurs were also early sea monsters. They lived from 210 to 65 million years ago in many parts of the world. Their name means "fish lizard" in Greek.

Ichthyosaurs also were not dinosaurs. They **evolved** from reptiles in the same way that seals and whales have evolved from land **mammals**.

Ichthyosaurs were marine reptiles with vertical tail fins and a narrow head. They were 7 to 30 feet long.

Skeletons have been found with babies inside them. Scientists believe that ichthyosaurs carried eggs inside their bodies until the eggs hatched. The babies were then born alive.

Could Nessie be a leftover plesiosaur or ichthyosaur? Who knows. Stranger things have happened.

CHAPTER 2

Coelacanth

It was December. The blazing sun beat down. The men worked the nets of their fishing boat. In most ways, it was like any other day. But one strange happening will forever set apart that day in 1938. It was the day a prehistoric fish came back to life.

The fishing boat was drifting off the southeast coast of Africa. The men pulled in the fishing net. They dumped its contents on the boat deck. Then they waded into the mass of slimy, squirming life.

The men quickly began to sort the fish. They threw those they didn't want back into the water. They had to work fast.

Suddenly, one of the men yelled as if he'd seen a ghost. The other fishermen gathered around. Oaths and shouts of surprise filled the air. A prehistoric monster was trapped in the nets!

No one had ever seen such a fish. Later, they learned that they had caught a coelacanth (SEE luh kanth).

The fish was 5 feet long and weighed 126 pounds. It had heavy steel-blue scales and bulgy eyes. Its fins looked like legs. That day, the fish lived out of the water about three hours.

The fish was very unusual. So the sea captain took it to a local museum. By the time the fish got to the museum, its insides were mush. All that was left was its skin. But the skin was enough to identify the fish as a coelacanth.

Until that December day in 1938, coelacanths were thought to have been **extinct** for 65 to 70 million years. Since then, several more coelacanths have been caught.

In 1998, a reef ecologist saw one while he was on his honeymoon in Indonesia. He was more than 6,000 miles from where the first coelacanth was found! The ecologist and his bride spotted the ugly fish in a market. His wife said it looked like something from an "alien" movie. Unfortunately, the fish was dead.

The ecologist knew that this was his chance to find a live coelacanth. He let it be known to local fishermen that he was in the market for a live one.

He didn't have to wait long. On July 30, 1998, a fisherman located a live coelacanth for the ecologist. It was 4 feet long and weighed 64 pounds. It was brown with white flecks. The fish was alive, but just barely.

They put the fish back in the ocean. The ecologist swam along beside it. He hoped to revive it. But it was too late. Sadly, the fish died.

The ecologist thinks the fish died from stress. It was used to swimming in deeper, cooler waters. The ecologist said, "It had these big, green **luminescent** eyes and seemed like such a gentle fish."

We still don't know very much about coelacanths. Early coelacanths were thought to be **ancestors** of the first **amphibians**. The structure of their limbs shows this. The coelacanth's skeleton is closely related to four-legged **vertebrates**.

Coelacanths have a deep, stocky body and a short, deep head. Their paired **dorsal** fins are rounded. The other fins are fan-shaped. The name *coelacanth* means "hollow spine" in Greek. We know coelacanths are **carnivorous**.

Few coelacanths have been found. Therefore, we don't know very much about them. But we believe one thing. Coelacanths are in danger of becoming extinct—for real this time.

CHAPTER 3

Sea Serpent

Sea serpents have been pesky problems since the dawn of time. Over 2,000 years ago, Virgil was busy writing about them. Virgil was the chief poet of his time. He lived in the Roman Empire.

Virgil was born in 70 B.C. He died in 19 B.C. He wrote the famous epic poem the *Aeneid*. His poetry is still printed and read today.

There are 12 books in the *Aeneid*. In the first two books, Virgil relates the story of the Trojan War. The story is told through the voice of Aeneas, the hero of the *Aeneid*. The story is part of Greek mythology.

The story tells how the Greeks had been trying to overcome the city of Troy for ten years. Finally, they brought a gigantic wooden horse to the city. There was a huge wall around Troy. The horse could only get inside if the Trojans opened the gate and let it in.

Some people were against accepting the wooden horse. They thought the big horse was a trick.

Laocoon was one of the men who thought it was a trick. He was a priest of Neptune, the god of the sea. Laocoon tried to keep his fellow countrymen from taking the wooden horse into the gates of Troy.

This is one version of Virgil's account of what happened.

After warning the people and sacrificing a steer to his god, Laocoon looked toward the sea. He spied two serpents. They were swimming side by side. As they moved, the sea divided. They were swept along by the swelling tides.

Their flaming heads showed above the waves. Their speckled tails steered their course. They climbed onto the land and strode across the plain.

Their wild eyes were filled with bloody streaks. And they licked their hissing jaws as they approached. Flames sputtered from their mouths.

Laocoon and his sons were amazed. They quickly fled. But they could not escape the monsters.

The serpents wound around the bodies of Laocoon's young boys. Then with their sharpened fangs, they ground the bodies.

Laocoon quickly ran to his sons' aid. But he was too late.

The serpents wound around his body twice. Twice around his waist their mass rolled. And twice about his gasping throat they folded. The priest was doubly choked.

13

Laocoon struggled to free himself. He tried to untie the knots around his body. His roars filled the air around him.

Finally, Laocoon and his altar were destroyed. The serpents left their prey. They made their way to the tower of Pallas. There they crouched at the feet of Athena, the goddess of war. They were protected by her.

It certainly didn't pay Laocoon to warn the people of Troy that the horse was dangerous! The giant sea serpents killed him and his sons in a very nasty way.

Stories about huge serpents appear throughout history. For example, there were several sightings along the New England coast in the early 1800s.

Four people in a boat saw what they first thought was a seal. Then they realized that the body was about 60 feet long! The monster approached their boat. The people could make out the head. It was larger than a horse's head. But it was shaped like a serpent's.

The monster was deep blue in color. It swam slowly toward them in an up-and-down motion. Before it reached their boat, it turned and swam away at great speed.

After this first sighting, many people saw the sea serpent all along the New England coast. Sea captains on ships saw the serpent. People strolling along shore also made sightings. And not all had heard the stories about other sightings. This made the sightings seem more believable. They didn't seem to be just cases of mass hysteria.

The sightings went on for many years. The monster was seen as far north as Nova Scotia. Many people saw the monster in the water. But it was never found. To this day, no one knows what the New England sea serpent really was.

There have been hundreds of giant sea serpent sightings in ages past. But we have no proof that such monsters ever lived. Today, scientists believe that people have confused at least three different sea animals with sea serpents.

The first possibility is the basking shark. There are about 375 different species of sharks. Some are big. Some are small. They come in shapes from flat and blunt to long and flexible. All sharks have skeletons made of cartilage.

Basking sharks grow to 50 feet long and weigh up to 5 tons. They are the second largest fish in the world. They are deep blue or charcoal in color.

Basking sharks have **gill rakers**. They sift their food and oxygen through the gill rakers as they swim along. They eat **plankton**.

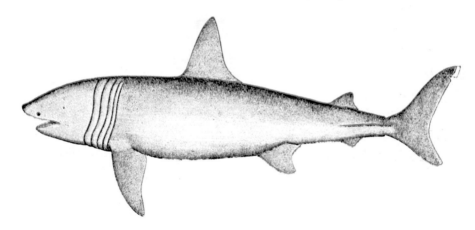

Basking sharks are lazy fellows. They never go over 3 miles per hour. They often lie still or bask on the water's surface. They are such slow swimmers and so often on the water's surface that they make an easy target for harpooners.

These sharks are killed for the oil in their livers. The oil is used to make cosmetics. Many have been killed. It is not known how many are left.

Basking sharks are usually seen alone or in pairs. But they have been known to gather in groups of 50 to 100.

They cruise along with their mouths open, filtering the water. In fact, 400,000 gallons of  water pass through a basking shark's mouth each hour.

In the winter, the water gets cold. And basking sharks disappear. No one knows for sure where they go. But it is thought that they go to the bottom of the ocean. They rest until the water warms up and the plankton reappears.

Most sharks produce a small number of eggs. But basking sharks produce 6 million. Each egg is about $1/5$ inch in diameter. Babies are about 5 feet long at birth.

Basking sharks are gentle fish that live in **temperate** waters in both the Northern and Southern Hemispheres. Their life span is not known.

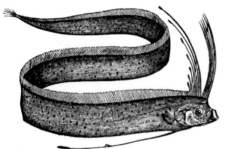

Another giant sea serpent look-alike is the oarfish. Oarfish are seldom seen unless they have washed ashore. Then they're probably sick or dead.

They live worldwide in temperate and **tropical** waters. Oarfish can grow to over 23 feet in length. They have flat, broad, ribbonlike bodies. And they are silver-blue or transparent with bright red fins. Little else is known about oarfish.

The third candidate for sea serpent is the sea snake. There are at least 50 species of front-fanged, poisonous sea snakes. They prefer warm, tropical oceans. They have long bodies, oarlike tails, nostrils on top of their heads, and salt glands. They sometimes bask by the thousands on the water's surface. They eat fish and eels, which they kill with their venom.

Strange as it may seem, most sea snakes are gentle and shy. They rarely bite people. In Japan, these snakes are smoked and eaten with soy sauce.

Which of the three candidates is the sea serpent from legends? Nobody knows for sure. What do you think?

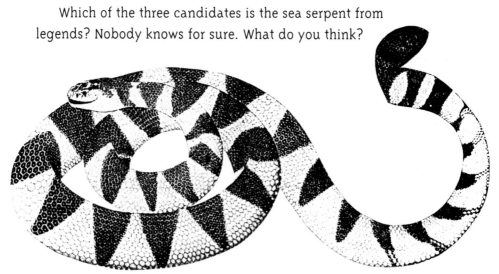

CHAPTER 4

Mermaid or Sirenian

You may disagree that a mermaid is a monster. But one definition of a monster is an "animal of unusual shape." And that would be a mermaid.

This is one version of *The Little Mermaid* by Hans Christian Andersen (1805–1875).

The Merking lived under the sea in a beautiful kingdom. He had six lovely daughters. Each was a mermaid.

As each daughter turned 15, she was allowed to swim to the top of the water. There she could see the sky, the land, and the world beyond.

The youngest daughter, however, longed to live in the world beyond the sea. Of course, she was the prettiest mermaid of all. She had a sweet voice. And she sang like an angel.

The youngest mermaid's fifteenth birthday finally came. She, too, swam to the surface of the water.

There she saw a huge ship. A big party was in progress. It was the prince's birthday. There were fireworks, dancing, and beautiful music.

The little mermaid had never seen anything so wonderful. All too soon it was time for her to return under the sea. But the little mermaid could not stop watching.

The evening wore on. A terrible storm came up. It tossed the ship against the rocks. It fell apart, and all the people drowned. All drowned but the prince.

The little mermaid rescued the prince. She swam with him to the edge of the water. She pushed him onto the shore. Then she swam away to watch him from a distance.

The next morning, a beautiful young girl walked along the shore. She found the prince and took him home.

The little mermaid returned home. But she kept thinking of the prince. She had fallen in love with him. And she could not forget him.

Finally, the mermaid's sisters went with her to find the prince's palace. They watched the prince from the water. The mermaid decided that she loved the prince too much to be apart from him. She must marry him.

The little mermaid went to the old witch's house. The old witch was a terrible person. Her house was built from the bones of people who had drowned. Its walls were slimy. The old witch was mean. But she agreed to help the little mermaid.

"You must do as I say," the old witch said. "I want your greatest gift in return for my help."

The witch continued. "Let me cut out your tongue. Then I can sing sweetly. And I'll give you something that will make you grow legs. You will be able to breathe on land. And you will meet the prince.

"You must make the prince marry you, though. If you don't, you will die. Then you will become sea foam. And you can never come back to the ocean. You will never see your family again."

You see, mermaids live for 300 years. But after that, they die and their souls turn into sea foam.

The little mermaid had to decide. Would she leave her family? Would she give up living for 300 years? Would she bear the pain of a knife cut? Would she give up her voice? Would she do all this to have a chance to marry the prince?

The little mermaid decided that she would give up all of this. Her love for the prince was very strong.

The little mermaid swallowed the witch's potion. She felt a sharp pain. Her tongue was cut out. Her tail became legs. Now she had the ability to live on land. But she could never speak again.

The little mermaid lay on the shore. The prince came walking along. He found her and took her to his castle.

The prince and the little mermaid became very close. But his love for her was more like a brother's love. He longed for the young girl who he thought had saved his life.

All the little mermaid could do was watch. She couldn't tell the prince that it was she who had saved him.

The king had arranged a marriage for the prince. When the prince met the young woman whom he was to marry, he was surprised. She was the same girl who had found him on the seashore after the little mermaid had saved him. The prince fell in love with the young woman. Very soon, they would be married.

The wedding took place on a ship. At the wedding party, the little mermaid danced and danced. No one had ever danced more beautifully. She knew that soon she would die and become sea foam. She had not fulfilled her wish to have the prince marry her.

As she danced, the little mermaid noticed some ugly animals swimming about in the water. When she looked closer, she realized that they were her sisters. Her sisters had given the witch their hair in exchange for the little mermaid's life.

"Here, sister," they said. "The witch has given us this knife. You must use it to stab the prince in the heart. When his blood flows onto your feet, you will become a mermaid again. You must do this now, before morning."

With that, the little mermaid's sisters handed her the knife and swam off.

The little mermaid looked at the knife. Then she looked at her beloved prince. He was asleep in the arms of his new wife. She threw the knife out into the ocean.

As the sun rose, the little mermaid turned to sea foam.

Today, people can view a statue of Andersen's Little Mermaid. It sits on a rock in the Copenhagen bay.

It is said that some sailors were at sea for so long that they forgot what women looked like. When they saw manatees swimming alongside the ship, they thought they were women with fish tails.

When you look at a manatee, it's hard to believe that sailors actually called them "mermaids."

In Greek mythology, there were creatures called *sirens*. They were female, partly human creatures whose singing lured sailors to their deaths. In the *Odyssey*, Ulysses stuffed his ears with beeswax to avoid being lured by the sirens.

In reality, sirens are manatees, dugongs, and the now extinct Steller's sea cow. Living sirenians—manatees and dugongs—are both found in warm, sheltered waters. They eat only sea plants.

Columbus saw sirens, or manatees, on his voyage to the New World. He wrote

I saw three sirens that came up very high out of the sea. They are not as beautiful as they are painted, since in some ways they have a face like a man.

Manatees are also called "sea cows." They grow up to 10 feet long. They can weigh 1,000 pounds. Their heavy, fishlike bodies end in a horizontally flattened fin. Their skin is gray and hairless. But they have a mustached face.

Manatees are sluggish and shy creatures. They spend their entire lives in the water.

There are three species of manatees—West Indian, West African, and Amazonian. The manatee is one of the most endangered marine mammals in U.S. waters.

Dugongs grow to about 11 feet long and weigh up to 880 pounds. Their tails are shaped like a **fluke**. They're like dolphins' tails.

Dugongs live in the western Pacific and Indian Oceans. There are more dugongs than manatees. But dugongs are also on the decline.

Manatee

Steller's sea cows lived in the North Pacific. They grew to 25 feet long and weighed 4 tons. Steller's sea cows were discovered in 1741. By 1768, they were extinct.

People wrote that they were good eating. And they were fairly easy to catch because they moved slowly.

Some people still hope that Steller's sea cows escaped extinction. They hope sea cows have built a new population. Once in a while, a sighting is reported. But so far, the sightings have all turned out to be whales.

CHAPTER 5

Leviathan

Leviathan (li VEYE uh thun) was a name used thousands of years ago for a big sea monster. Leviathans have been associated with dragons, crocodiles, sea serpents, and whales. Crocodiles don't live in the sea. And the other creatures don't really exist. So to simplify things, that leaves whales as the leviathans of ancient times.

Moby Dick was written by Herman Melville and published in 1851. Many say that it is the best-known whale story. And many think it is one of the best novels ever written.

"Call me Ishmael" is how the story begins. Ishmael is the narrator. The story is about a great sperm whale named Moby Dick. In a nutshell, Ishmael's story goes something like this.

I went down to the seaside town of New Bedford. I had plans to join a whaling ship. I found an inn to stay in until I had a job. The inn was full. So I had to share a room.

When I met my roommate, he gave me quite a shock. His name was Queequeg. He stood over six and a half feet tall. He had tattoos all over his body. And he made his living selling shrunken heads.

Despite our differences, Queequeg and I became good friends. We decided to sign up on the same whaling ship, the Pequod. *The captain of the ship was Captain Ahab.*

On the chosen day, we set sail. The Pequod was a beautiful old wooden ship. She had tall masts and billowing white sails.

In the beginning, the skies were blue. There was a good breeze. The crew took turns climbing the masts and searching the ocean for whales.

One day, one of the mates yelled, "There she blows!"

Off the **starboard** side of the ship we saw a whale. We lowered the small boats and rowed toward the whale. The harpooners stood at the front of the boats. They aimed their **harpoons**.

When we were near enough, the harpoons flew toward the whale. They speared it in the back. Then we went for what we called a "Nantucket sleigh ride."

The speared whale swam on. It pulled our small boats through the ocean. It was the ship's job to keep up with us.

After a long ride, the whale tired and finally died.

On the deck, we cut up the whale's body. We stripped the blubber and boiled out the oil. The oil would be used to burn lamps and to keep people warm. As we worked, one of the mates kept watch for another whale.

During all this time, we hadn't yet seen our captain. Sometimes we'd hear Captain Ahab at night. He would pace the deck above our sleeping quarters. We knew it was him because of his ivory leg.

We'd been told that Captain Ahab had lost his leg during a whaling venture. He had used a whale bone to replace it. The whale that took Ahab's leg was a great white whale. His name was Moby Dick.

Finally, Captain Ahab called the men together. He offered a Spanish ounce of gold to the man who first saw Moby Dick. The captain nailed the gold piece to the main mast as a reminder.

All the captain cared about was finding the great white whale. And he took great pains to find Moby Dick.

Whales migrate all over the globe. And Captain Ahab knew
Moby Dick's route. He even plotted our course especially to cross
Moby Dick's path. He didn't mind that we might miss a dozen
whales by taking a different course.

We came upon several whalers in our journey. Then one day,
we came upon the Rachel. The ship had found Moby Dick.

During the fight, the captain of the Rachel had lost his son at
sea. He pleaded with Ahab to help find his boy.

Ahab said "No." We had to chase Moby Dick.

Captain Ahab set course for where the Rachel had been.

A great storm came up. Our sails were torn in the winds. In
the midst of the storm, Ahab ordered us to put up new sails. We
were going to keep sailing in the storm!

Then one
day as I was
on lookout
duty, I
spotted a
whale. I
yelled, "There
she blows!"
Then I
saw more
whales.
There must
have been a hundred! This was our chance to make our voyage
successful.

As soon as we killed enough whales, we could return home.
But Ahab said to keep going. Forget about the whales. He was only
after one whale—Moby Dick.

We sailed on in search of the great whale. At one time, there
was no wind to move our ship. For days, we had nothing to do. It
was hot. There was not a breeze. The sun beat down all day.

We entertained ourselves with games and stories. Or we found a spot of shade and slept.

One day, Queequeg was telling his own fortune. A strange look came over his face. He had seen his own death. And it was horrible. He called for the carpenter to build him a coffin. Then he sat waiting for death. He wouldn't talk, eat, or sleep.

Queequeg sat that way for many hot, still days. Out of boredom one day, some men took a knife and carved lines in his skin. They added new designs to his many tattoos.

The knife cut deep into his flesh. But Queequeg didn't flinch. I tried to get the knife away from the men. We fought and they almost killed me. But Queequeg came out of his trance and wrestled the knife from the men.

After that, he moved about and did his job. By this time, though, his coffin was waiting for him.

Finally, the winds picked up. We came upon a ghost ship with the unfitting name of Delight. The ship was in tatters. Most of the men had been killed. The white whale had met the Delight and done its job.

On a day shortly after our meeting with the Delight, we heard the cry we'd all been dreading. "There she blows! There she blows! A hump like a snow-hill! It is Moby Dick!"

We prepared to fight the battle. The boats were lowered. The men rowed out. Captain Ahab was in one of the boats. Moby Dick raised out of the water under Ahab's boat. It capsized. The great whale's jaw snapped the boat in half. Then the whale circled the boat.

The other boats stayed out of the way.

Ahab spotted the Pequod not far off.

"Sail on the whale! Drive him off!" he yelled. The Pequod did just that. Finally, the whale and his victims were separated. Ahab was pulled into another boat.

Night came. We had to wait until morning to continue the chase.

The next day, we found Moby Dick again. This time we were able to harpoon him. He swam on with the harpoons in his back and ropes all around him. All three boats followed him on a Nantucket sleigh ride. The big whale twisted and turned. Our ropes wound round and round him.

Captain Ahab's boat was demolished. His ivory peg was broken off.

Again the Pequod came to the rescue. Dusk came again. Moby Dick was still in sight, tied to us by the lines.

On the third day, the crew in the Pequod could see Moby Dick's wake. Once again the boats were lowered. Once again, we rowed off after the big whale.

Sharks appeared all around. They were drawn by the whale's blood. The huge whale darted around, fighting the boats.

In the battle, a harpoon line got caught around one of the men. He flew overboard with the harpoon and became tacked to Moby Dick's back.

The great whale rose out of the water. The dead man's eyes stared straight at Captain Ahab.

Moby Dick rammed the Pequod again and again. At last, the old ship and all her men sank to the bottom of the sea. In the swelling waters of the sinking ship, the other boats were pulled down too. All were lost. Queequeg's vision had come true.

I alone remained on top of the water. As the sea boiled over the Pequod, Queequeg's coffin burst out of the water. I grabbed it and clung to it.

I was picked up by the Rachel, the ship whose captain had asked for Ahab's help in finding his son. But the Rachel, "in her retracing search for her missing children, had only found another orphan."

So ends the tale of the great sperm whale, Moby Dick.

There are presently two kinds of whales—baleen and toothed whales. Baleen whales eat plankton, krill, and other small things in the ocean.

They swim along with their mouths open, straining their food from the sea.

Baleen whales have two blowholes. In the past, baleens have been hunted to use in products such as ladies' whalebone corsets.

Baleen whales include blue whales, humpback whales, right whales, gray whales, and fin whales.

Blue whales are the largest known animals that have ever lived. They grow to 100 feet and weigh more than 118 tons.

Toothed whales are predators. They feed on fish and squid. The family of toothed whales includes dolphins and porpoises.

Pilot whales, belugas or white whales, killer whales, pygmy sperm whales, and sperm whales also belong to this group.

Sperm whales can grow to 62 feet. They are recognized by their large, oblong head and narrow lower jaw.

About one-third of a sperm whale's body is its head. A good part of its large head is filled with an oily substance. It is thought that the oily substance acts as a cushion against the great pressure that the whale feels in its deep dives.

Sperm whales have been known to dive more than a mile deep. They can stay underwater for an hour or longer.

Sperm whales can eat more than a ton of food a day. They especially like squid and cuttlefish.

Signs of fierce battles with giant squid have been found on many sperm whales' bodies. It is easy to see where a giant squid's suction cups have cut into a whale's flesh, both inside the stomach and outside on the skin.

Whales are torpedo-shaped. Their front flippers are used for stabilizing or steering. They move through the water using up-and-down movements of their tails and flukes.

Under a whale's skin is a dense layer of blubber. It maintains its body temperature at 93° to 97°F. Because they are air-breathing mammals, whales must rise to the surface to breathe.

The blowhole on the left side near the front of a whale's head is its nostril. This is where air escapes. What looks like water or steam coming from a blowhole is actually a whale's used air.

Not much is known about breeding habits of whales. But the **gestation period** for sperm whales is thought to be about 16 months. Their young are born alive and nursed for about a year. The life span of whales is from 30 to 90 years.

Whales migrate all over the world. They have certain paths they follow. This is probably due to ocean currents, temperatures, and other environmental factors.

Whales travel in groups called *schools*, *pods*, or *gams*. In times past, before the number of whales was so depleted, a pod would be hundreds of whales. But

nowadays, pods are made up of fewer animals.

Whales communicate through sound. Sperm whales produce short, pulse-like sounds that are used for **echolocation**. They use these sounds to help locate food. Sound waves travel through the water. When they hit something, the sound waves bounce back to the whale. There are also high-pitched sounds that seem to be more social in nature.

Sperm whales are the most abundant of the great whales. There are probably a half million sperm whales. But three times as many sperm whales once roamed the earth.

CHAPTER 6

Kaahu-pahau and Megamouth

Sharks were revered and dreaded by ancient peoples. There are time-worn tales of sharks in many cultures.

Ancient Hawaiians built shark pens in bays or harbors. They lined edges of the bay with huge lava stones. Water could flow in and out. But once sharks got in, they were trapped.

One such pen was near the island of Oahu. It was near today's city of Honolulu. When the navy dug up Pearl Harbor to make the sea base there, they destroyed an ancient shark pen.

You've heard of **matadors**. Well, the Hawaiians had their own version.

The Hawaiians built shark pens. Then they trapped sharks and starved them.

When the sharks were hungry, warriors entered the pen. They would fight the sharks.

The only weapon a warrior had was a knife. It was made from a single shark's tooth.

When a shark charged, the warrior would dive suddenly. From underneath, he would try to rip the shark's belly open with the knife.

Ancient Hawaiian legends tell of men killing sharks in this way. Even so, it's hard to believe that a man could be quick or strong enough to kill a shark with only one shark's tooth.

Sometimes humans were thrown to the hungry sharks. Ancient Hawaiians thought great blue sharks were special. One was the "Queen Shark," named Kaahu-pahau. She lived at the bottom of the shark pen. She and her brother guarded the waters against man-eating sharks. To keep her happy, human offerings were sometimes made.

A few years ago, an interesting Hawaiian shark adventure happened. In November of 1976, the navy was doing research about 25 miles off the coast of Oahu. They were working 15,000 feet underwater. A strange creature swallowed their sea anchor at about 660 feet. They pulled up a dead shark. But this wasn't just any shark. It had a big, glowing mouth that was three feet wide! It was 16 feet long and weighed 1,653 pounds. No one had ever seen this type of shark before. They named it "megamouth."

Megamouths live in deep waters. They use their luminescent big mouths to lure krill and other small creatures.

Since 1976, a few more megamouth sharks have been found off the coast of southern California, near Australia, and near Japan.

In 1990, scientists discovered a living megamouth off the coast of California. They attached a radio tag to it. Then scientists could track the shark.

They found that it spent daytime hours in water 450 to 500 feet deep. At night, it followed its food source up to about 40 feet deep.

We don't know how many megamouth sharks there are. There's still a lot we don't know about megamouths. And there could be other sharks out there that we haven't even met!

CHAPTER 7

Jenny Haniver, Basilisk, or Devilfish

Jenny Hanivers have been popular sea monsters from the mid-1500s through the 20th century. In fact, you may still find Jenny in some seaside shops today.

No one knows where the name *Jenny Haniver* came from. Perhaps she was the first person to fashion a Jenny Haniver.

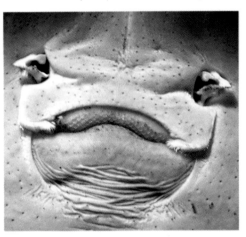

You see, a Jenny Haniver is a **ray** or **skate** that has been cut apart, shaped into a little "monster," and dried.

A ray's underside looks like a person's face. Some Jenny Hanivers looked like very ugly people.

Others looked more like dragons.

Some people believe that Jenny Hanivers and **basilisks** are one and the same. The basilisk is a sea monster of legend. At one time, it was described as a serpent. In 1613, basilisks were described as monstrous flying fish. And little, dried-out Jenny Haniver became proof of their existence.

Rays are related to sharks and skates. They have broad, flat, winglike fins along the sides of their heads. Their tails are like

whips. Their eyes and **spiracles** are on top of their heads. Their mouths and gill slits are underneath.

Manta rays are the largest of the rays. These rays can be as big as 22 feet wide and weigh 3,000 to 4,000 pounds. Manta rays live in tropical waters worldwide. But some have been found as far north as New England, Spain, Japan, or California.

Manta is Spanish for *cloak*. These rays look like flying cloaks or blankets. Their bodies are diamond-shaped. And they have thin, whiplike tails.

A manta ray's skin changes shades with age. It changes from a reddish color to an olive-brown to black.

They swim as if they are flying. Their fins have cartilage just like we have in our noses and ears.

Mantas have **cephalic** fins on each side of their heads in front of their mouths. They are used to direct food into their mouths. Their diet consists of plankton, shrimp, and small fish.

Food is filtered from the water with special **gill arches**. Then the water is pumped out on the bottom side of the mantas. They use this same system for breathing. Manta rays feed in deep water, midway between the surface and the bottom.

Manta rays are gentle creatures. Their spiny tails are not poisonous. Divers sometimes grab onto them and swim with the rays.

Fishermen do not fish for mantas, even though they are good to eat. Mantas put up a terrific fight when they are pulled from the water. They can damage or even sink boats.

Manta rays sometimes leap into the air. They land on the water with a huge smack. We don't know why they do this. One theory is that this is the manta ray's way of ridding its body of little parasites. Perhaps mantas are just scratching an itch. Because of this strange habit, manta rays have earned the name of *devilfish*.

Manta rays hatch from eggs inside their mothers. They are then born alive. One baby is born at a time. It can weigh up to 20 pounds and is 4 feet across. The baby feeds on milk from its mother.

The life span of manta rays is not known.

CHAPTER 8

Hydra or Polyp

The hydra was a nine-headed sea monster of Greek legend. If one head was cut off, another grew in its place. So it was almost impossible to kill the hydra.

Hercules solved the problem by burning eight of the hydra's heads. Then he buried the ninth under a rock.

In the Vatican, there is a marble tablet that shows the story of "Hercules and the Hydra." The artist made the hydra look remarkably like an octopus. Today, we believe that the hydra of myth was indeed an octopus.

Pliny the Elder lived during the first century A.D. He lumped squids and octopuses together under the term *polyp*. This is how Pliny's description of an octopus is interpreted.

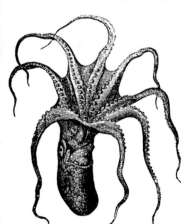

No animal is more savage in causing the death of a man in the water. It attacks men who have been shipwrecked or are diving. The polyp struggles with him by coiling around him. Then it swallows the man with its sucker-cups and drags him to pieces by its multiple suction. But it should be noted that a polyp's strength gets weaker when it is lying stretched out on its back.

About 150 years ago, another story about the octopus became well known.

"Religion, society, and nature; these are the three struggles of humanity," wrote Victor Hugo in 1866. You may have heard of Hugo's work. He wrote *The Hunchback of Notre Dame* (1831). It is about the struggle with religion. He also wrote *Les Misérables* (1862). It describes the struggle with society. And his third novel, *Toilers of the Sea* (1866), deals with the struggle with nature.

Hugo's purpose for writing this book was to show the *toil*, or labor. He chose the sea as his setting. It was the Channel Islands in the English Channel, to be exact.

The hero of the book is a strong, hardworking young man. His name is Gilliatt. Gilliatt is an outcast. That's because his mother is thought to be a witch.

As the story begins, the steamship *Durande* is wrecked in a terrible hurricane. Gilliatt is in love with the owner's daughter. He wants to prove that he is worthy of her. So Gilliatt agrees to **salvage** the steam engine from the terrible reef of Douvres.

The job is almost impossible. But Gilliatt's strength is superhuman. After much hard work, he gets the job done. But that's not the end of the story.

After all that effort, Gilliatt was very hungry. So he went back to the water to catch a crab for supper. He thrust his hand into a crack between some rocks.

All at once, he felt himself seized by the arm. He could not describe the horror he felt.

*Something thin, rough, flat, slimy, sticky, and living had just wound itself round his bare arm. It crept up toward his chest. It was like the pressure of a leather thong. And it had the thrust of a **gimlet**.*

In less than a second, a strange spiral form had passed around his wrist and elbow. It reached to his shoulder. The point crept under his armpit.

Gilliatt threw himself backward. But he could hardly move. It was as though he were nailed to the spot. Only his left hand remained free. He took his knife, which he held between his teeth.

Holding the knife with his hand, he braced himself against the rock. Gilliatt tried desperately to move his right arm. He only succeeded in slightly moving the bond that held him. It was as soft as leather, solid as steel, and cold as night.

A second thong sprung from the rocks. It, too, was narrow and pointed. It was like a tongue from the jaws of a monster. It licked Gilliatt's body in a terrible way.

Suddenly, it stretched out, immensely long and thin. It applied itself to his skin and surrounded his whole body. Gilliatt's suffering was comparable to nothing he had known before.

On his skin, Gilliatt felt something round and horrible. It seemed to him that countless lips were fastened to his flesh. And they were seeking to drink his blood.

A third thong snaked outside the crack. It felt for Gilliatt and lashed his sides like a cord. It fixed itself there.

Pain and suffering are silent when at their highest point. Gilliatt did not utter a cry. There was enough light for him to see the dreadful forms sticking to him.

A fourth thong appeared. This one was as swift as a dart. It leaped toward his belly and rolled itself around.

It was impossible to tear or cut away these shiny thongs. They were stuck closely to Gilliatt's body by sucking points.

Each of these points was the source of frightful and peculiar pain. It was like being swallowed all at once by a throng of mouths that were too small.

A fifth thong leaped from the hole. It flung itself upon the others and folded over Gilliatt's chest. Crushing pressure was added to horror. Gilliatt could hardly breathe.

These thongs spread out gradually like the blades of swords. All five evidently belonged to the same center. They crept and crawled over Gilliatt. He felt these strange points of pressure. They felt like hundreds of mouths. And they were changing their places.

Suddenly a large, round, flat, slimy mass rose from the lower part of the crack.

It was the center. The five thongs were attached to it like spokes to a hub. On the opposite side of this evil disk, Gilliatt could see three other **tentacles**. But for now they remained under the rock.

In the middle of this sliminess, there were two eyes gazing right at Gilliatt.

Gilliatt recognized the octopus. He knew it was cunning. Also he knew it would try to shock its prey at first. Then it would grab hold and wait.

Gilliatt held his knife. The suction increased.

He gazed at the octopus. It stared right back at him.

All at once, the creature detached its sixth tentacle from the rock and launched it at Gilliatt. It tried to grab his left arm.

At the same time, it thrust its head forward swiftly. A second more and its mouth would have been applied to Gilliatt's chest. If that had happened, Gilliatt would have been a dead man.

But Gilliatt was on his guard. Being watched, he watched.

He avoided the tentacle. And at the moment the creature was about to bite his chest, he dropped his armed fist on the monster.

Gilliatt plunged the point of his knife into the flat, slimy mass. With a twisting movement, he carved a circle around the two eyes. Then he tore out the head as one might pull out a tooth.

It was finished.

The whole creature dropped.

It resembled a sheet floating to the ground. The air pump had been destroyed. So the vacuum no longer existed. All at once, some four hundred suckers released their hold of the rock and the man.

The octopus sank to the bottom.

Gilliatt was panting from the battle. He could see on the rocks at his feet two shapeless, jellylike masses. The head was on one side. The rest was on the other. (We say "the rest," because one could not say the body.)

Gilliatt, however, feared a return of the pain. So he retreated beyond the reach of the tentacles.

But the monster was really dead.

Gilliatt closed his knife.

Of course, this isn't the end of the story. But since it's the end of the octopus, we'll stop here.

Pliny, Hugo, and others gave octopuses a bad reputation. Octopuses are actually gentle, shy creatures.

There are many truths in Hugo's description of the octopus. There are also some fictions. It is true that octopuses live all over the world. But most are no bigger than 2 feet long. There are more than 150 varieties of octopus.

Never mind that giant octopuses don't really live in the English Channel. They inhabit the Pacific Ocean from the Sea of Japan to Alaska and California. They live in the rocky sea bottom.

Hugo called them, "A glutinous mass possessed of a will . . . Glue filled with hatred."

Octopuses may be the smartest sea creatures that are not mammals. But they are shy and don't prey on people. They can figure out how to open a jar to get what's inside. And if you leave an octopus in an aquarium and put clams or another tasty treat in a nearby aquarium, you won't have your clams for long. The octopus will crawl out of its aquarium and join its dinner in the other.

The *Guinness Book of World Records* lists a giant octopus at 31 feet long and 600 pounds. That was a big octopus!

Most giant octopus males can weigh 100 pounds or more. And females weigh about 60 pounds.

An octopus's head and body are joined so that they appear to be one large bulb. Actually, the head is just the part around the eyes. The rest is mostly stomach.

Octopuses have eight tentacles, or arms. Each arm has two rows of suckers on the underside. Giant octopuses have 2,000 suckers.

The tentacles find food and determine water conditions. They can tell shapes, textures, and tastes. The suckers are also used for gripping rocks and anchoring the octopus to things.

Giant octopuses are *nocturnal*. That means they roam at night and sleep during the day. They live alone. Octopuses are very strong. But they tire quickly.

An octopus is covered with a skin called a **mantle**. Underneath the mantle is the **mantle cavity**. It's like a siphon or funnel.

To swim, the octopus sucks water into the mantle cavity. Then it shoots the water out through the funnel. This method makes the octopus swim very fast. It can move forward, backward, and sideways. The octopus also walks along the ocean floor on its arms.

Octopuses eat by using their suckers to find prey. They then wrap their arms around the food. They eat clams, mussels, cockles, lobsters, sea snails, and fish.

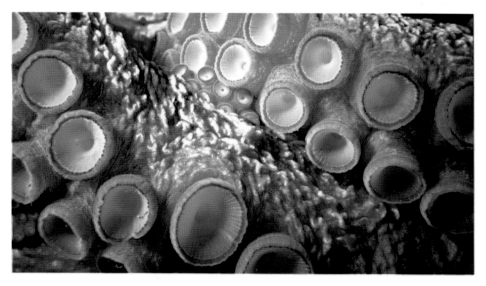

Different octopuses have different favorite foods. Scientists have found lobster shells outside one octopus's cave, clam shells by another, and so on. People have even seen octopuses reach out of the water and grab seagulls from the shore.

An octopus's arms push food into its mouth. The octopus has a **radula**. This is a beak and a toothed tongue. The octopus uses it to crush food. Poison is injected into the prey when it is bitten.

Predators of giant octopuses include seals, sharks, and other giant octopuses. In fact, just about everything likes to eat them. They use their arms, suckers, and radulae to defend themselves.

Octopuses can change colors to hide. When they are mad, they turn red. To blend with the surroundings, octopuses can turn tan, brown, gray, or green. When they are scared, they turn white. And when they are very excited, they turn a variety of colors in a patterned display. Even baby octopuses in their egg sacs can change colors!

Octopuses squirt out clouds of brown ink to leave their predators in the dark. Then they make quick getaways.

What if an enemy bites off an octopus's arm? The octopus can grow another, shorter arm!

Octopuses feel like jelly. They have a slimy and wiggly feeling. They have no bones. So they can squeeze into very small places. That's all the better for hiding.

They have advanced-type eyes. They have eyelids, corneas, irises, moveable lenses, and retinas. Their pupils are long strips instead of dots like ours.

Octopuses can turn their eyes 180°. Therefore, they don't have to move their heads to look behind themselves.

After a male and female have mated, the male dies. The female produces about 100,000 eggs. She attaches them to the roof of her cave. They hang there in strings that look like rice.

The mother takes good care of her eggs. She cleans them and blows fresh saltwater over them. She watches over them for six months. She never leaves them. During this time she doesn't eat. She dies of starvation just after her eggs hatch.

The young octopuses are very small. They swim with the plankton. Many get eaten by fish. Those that survive finally settle to the bottom of the ocean. They mature at one year. They live to be about three years old.

Octopuses are harmless to people. In fact, the expert diver Max Gene Nohl has said, "The chance of a diver being attacked by an octopus is as remote as the possibility of a hunter in the woods being attacked by a rabbit." Most octopuses are just curious.

The only really dangerous octopuses are tiny blue-ringed octopuses. They have poison bites that can kill a person in minutes. They live in tide pools in the South Pacific.

All in all, we are much more dangerous to octopuses than they are to us.

CHAPTER 9

Kraken

*O*laus Magnus described krakens in his history of Sweden in 1555. Before that, something similar to krakens was described in the *Odyssey*. It is thought that krakens were probably giant squids. Or they could have been octopuses. Back then, people didn't know the difference.

In 1870, Jules Verne wrote *Twenty Thousand Leagues Under the Sea*. In this science fiction thriller, Captain Nemo, captain of the *Nautilus*, a submarine that was way ahead of its time, is set on destroying the world.

The time is the late 1860s. The place is the South Seas. The story is told by Professor Aronnax from the Paris Museum. Professor Aronnax and two other men are being held against their wills on the *Nautilus*.

The *Nautilus* attacks ships from under water. In the story, the *Nautilus* itself is thought to be a sea monster.

In one chapter, the *Nautilus* is attacked by a giant squid. This retelling describes Professor Aronnax's version.

It was a giant squid. And it was 25 feet long. It was heading toward the Nautilus, *swimming backward very fast. Its huge immobile eyes were of a blue-green color. The eight arms, or rather legs, were coming out of its head. It is this which has earned it the name of "cephalopod." They were twice as long as its body and were twisting about like the hair of a Greek fury.*

We could clearly make out the 250 suckers lining the inside of its tentacles. Some had already fastened onto the glass panel of the lounge.

This monster's mouth was a horny beak that looked like that of a parakeet. It opened and closed vertically.

Its tongue was also made of a hornlike substance. It was armed with several rows of sharp teeth. It would come out and shake what seemed like veritable cutlery. What a whim of nature! A bird's beak in a **mollusk**!

Its elongated body had a slight swelling in the middle. It formed a fleshy mass that must have weighed between 40 and 50 thousand pounds. Its color seemed to change very fast, according to the animal's mood. It varied from a ghastly gray to reddish brown. To think they possess three hearts!

Jules Verne's description of the giant squid is on target, with a few small exceptions. Of course, Jules Verne's story is fiction.

A giant squid has never been known to attack people, except for one report. In the early 1870s, *The Times*, a London newspaper, had such a story. It reported that the schooner *Pearl* was sunk in the Bay of Bengal by a giant squid. The ship's captain had shot at the squid. Over 100 witnesses saw the attack. It is thought that the squid probably mistook the ship for its enemy, the sperm whale. Isn't it interesting that this account occurred shortly after *Twenty Thousand Leagues Under the Sea* was published?

Then in 1875, the crew aboard the ship *Pauline* saw a whale fighting a giant sea monster. For about 15 minutes, the men watched. Something (probably tentacles) picked the whale up out of the water. It then dragged the whale below the surface. This monster could only have been a giant squid.

Giant squids are one of 300 species of squids. They live on the bottom of the North Atlantic Ocean from 1,000 to 3,000 feet deep. Sometimes they can be seen on the surface of the ocean.

Their bodies can grow up to 5 feet in diameter and average 15 to 25 feet long. Giant squids are the world's largest living **invertebrate**. Their tentacles can be 30 to 35 feet long. From tail to tip, giant squids can be 60 feet long. Giant squids have been known to weigh 1,000 pounds.

Giant squids' bodies are shaped like torpedoes. They taper toward the tail end. On either side of their bodies, toward the tail, are fins for swimming.

Their neck, head, and body are all parts of the torpedo shape. They have excellent vision in their large, round eyes. In fact, their eyes are the largest eyes of any animal. They are as big around as a car's headlights. They produce light to help squids see in the dark ocean depths.

Attached to the head in front of the eyes are eight long, slender, round tentacles with many suckers and hoods. The tentacles are used for moving around.

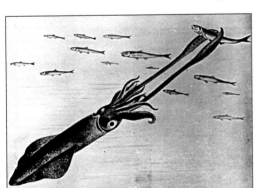

Two more tentacles are longer. They don't have suckers or hoods, except near the tips. These tentacles are used for catching prey.

Like octopuses, giant squids have mantles and mantle cavities. There is an opening to

the mantle in the head and back. The openings are called *funnels*. Squids move by opening one funnel, closing the other, and squeezing the mantle cavity closed. This moves squids forward or backward very quickly. They breathe through gills.

Squids also shoot ink into the air to confuse attackers. And, like octopuses, they can change colors quickly. Deepwater squid also can create their own light. They make the same pale green light that fireflies produce.

Giant squids hide near the bottom of the ocean. They wait for their prey to happen by. The two longest tentacles are kept coiled near their mouths.

Then when prey passes, a squid shoots those tentacles out. They seize the fish or other animal. Then the tentacles pass the food to one of the eight arms. The arm feeds the mouth.

The giant squid's beak is like that of a parrot. It crushes the bones and shells of its prey.

The female hatches several hundred eggs a few weeks after breeding.

It is also believed that giant squids live alone. But squids often hunt in packs. Little else is known about giant squids because they are rarely seen. They are even more rarely studied.

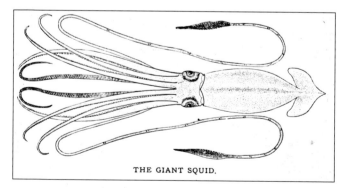

THE GIANT SQUID.

Epilogue

So one question remains. Are there sea monsters? The "sea monsters" in this book represent just a fraction of the strange creatures in our oceans. Remember, too, that we're still discovering new life. Think about the coelacanth or the megamouth. It is very possible that some weird, unknown creatures are lurking in the deepest, darkest parts of the ocean.

Do these sea monster stories remind you of anything? What about all the space aliens that we see in movies and read about in science fiction books? Of course, they are ideas from people's imaginations. So were the monsters in this book, at one time.

Do you suppose there is life elsewhere? In our exploration of space, will we encounter monsters? Or will we meet creatures from different worlds that are really no stranger than some of the sea monsters?

Time will tell. It always does.

Glossary

amphibian . . . . class of cold-blooded animals such as frogs that have gills when young and breathe air when adults

ancestor . . . . . . forefather; one who comes before

basilisk . . . . . . legendary reptile with fatal breath and glance

carnivorous . . . . meat-eating

cephalic . . . . . . situated on or near the head

cephalopod . . . . class of marine mollusks (see separate glossary entry), including the squids and octopuses, that expel water from a tube under the head, have tentacles, highly developed eyes, and a sac containing ink

curator . . . . head of a museum, zoo, or art gallery

dorsal . . . . situated on or near the back

echolocation . . . process for locating distant objects by means of sound waves

evolve . . . . to change over time

extinct . . . . no longer existing

fluke . . . . one of the lobes on a whale's tail

gestation period . length of time between conception and birth

gill arch . . . . . . bony, curved bar that supports the gills of fish and amphibians

gill raker . . . . . bony processor on a gill arch (see separate glossary entry) that guides solid substances away from the gills

gimlet . . . . . . small tool with a cross handle and screw point; used for boring holes

harpoon . . . . . . barbed spear used in hunting large fish or whales

invertebrate . . . lacking a spinal column, or backbone

Jurassic period . . time when the dinosaurs lived; over 200 million years ago

kraken . . . . . . Scandinavian sea monster

luminescent . . . glowing from light produced by a chemical process in the body

mammal . . . . . . class of warm-blooded animals whose young are born alive and are nourished by milk from the female

mantle . . . . . . soft, external body wall

mantle cavity . . space inside the mantle

marine . . . . . . relating to the sea

matador . . . . . . principal bullfighter who kills the bull

mollusk . . . . . . invertebrate with a soft unsegmented body, usually enclosed in a shell

plankton . . . . . . tiny animal and plant life that floats or swims weakly in a body of water

polyp . . . . creature with a hollow, round body and a central mouth surrounded by tentacles with suckers

predator . . . . . animal that hunts, kills, and devours others

radula . . . . . . horny band that has minute teeth that tear up food and draws it into the mouth

ray . . . . an order of fish that have flattened bodies

reptile . . . . air-breathing vertebrate that has scales and crawls on its belly or with short legs, such as snakes, alligators, lizards

salvage . . . . recover something valuable from wreckage

shanghai . . . . to put aboard a ship by force

skate . . . . any of a family of rays that have a flat diamond shape

spiracle . . . . . breathing hole

starboard . . . . right side of a ship

temperate . . . . having to do with a moderate climate

tentacle . . . . . long, flexible extension close to the head that resembles an arm and is used for grasping and feeling

tropical . . . . . having to do with a climate that is hot and moist

vertebrate . . . . having a spinal column, or backbone

Index